Dedication

*To my grandmother, Geraldine,
who shared with me her gift for telling
stories.*

Contents

Acknowledgements

In order for me to end up a Global Citizen, my travels had to start somewhere. My mom was my first traveling companion or maybe it was the other way around. Nonetheless, in 1963 when I was 4 years old, my mom made a trip from New York City to Detroit with my younger sister and myself. It was my first time on an airplane and while I would love to tell you that I remember all of the exciting details about my first flight, I don't think I will be able to do that.

When my mom told me the story about our first flight together, I thought to myself that sounded just like me. She recounted that my younger sister was just a toddler, so she was focused on getting her on the airplane and situated. All the while, I was next to my mom so that she could keep an eye on me.

She told me that I walked on the plane confidently, yet I seemed curious about it. She explained that I spoke to the 'stewardesses' as we boarded and that when I got to my seat, I just jumped into it like I knew what I was doing. On my first flight and for most of my flights that followed, I was a window guy. I loved looking out at everything on the ground before we took off and then seeing all the clouds and the blue sky as the plane took flight.

Since my first flight with my mom at the young age of 4, we have gone on to travel together on countless flights to some amazing destinations. I am grateful to my mom for giving me the flying experience at such a young age and for allowing me to find one of my life's passions so early on. It's exciting to recall something in your life, that brings you so much happiness.

I want to thank Michael Flores, my husband, for his unconditional love that shows up in the most amazing ways. During our engagement and for the first 4 years of our marriage, my travels away from home exceeded the time I was there. Most of the time when I was home during this period, I truly felt like I was on a constant layover. My suitcase was rarely put away and my packing skills were honed to the point that I could fill my suitcase in under 15 minutes no matter how long my trip was going to be.

He was supportive of me and my career and showed it with little gestures and not so little gestures. There were plenty of times when I would get to my hotel room in some remote part of China and, while unpacking my suitcase I would find a hand written note from Michael encouraging me and telling me that he was waiting for me at home with the pups.

I remember the time when I was talking with the flight attendants in the galley during a trans-Atlantic flight and told them that Michael drops me off and picks me up for every flight. They were impressed and told me that he was giving me what they called "princess service". I had never heard that term before and it made me feel special. I told Micheal when he picked me up from that trip that I was grateful for the "princess service". He dropped me off and picked me up at all hours of the day and night, I am grateful for him.

There was no better feeling than the one that I had knowing he was the last person I would see when I left and the first person I would see when I returned home. He made the best of our time together. While I was home, he would push me to relax and rest which I really needed and was not very good at. I did do my best to have a nice dinner with him on the nights before I left on any trip. It became one of our special memory making experiences while I was traveling so much of the time.

The idea for this book came to me while reflecting on all of the amazing experiences that I had while flying with some of the best flight attendants in the industry. I am grateful to the women and men who chose this as their primary career. There are several common traits amongst almost every one of them, who I had the pleasure of flying with over the years.

Flight attendants have taught me a lot about life during my time on airplanes with them. I remember learning my first lesson about time management from them. While I had always been very organized with my time, it was impressive to see the flight attendants prepare for landing after the 2 chimes signal from the cockpit. They were able to get so much done throughout the cabin and in the galley in a matter of minutes. They ended up in their jump seats with time to spare.

The stories in this book would not have been possible without the flight attendants who I met and befriended over the years. While many people give little, if any, attention to them or worse, treat them rudely and disrespectfully; I have massive gratitude for them and for everything that they have done for me over the years. I saw them earn their wings on every flight.

I joined a frequent flyer program for the first time in 1987 while attending a travel and tourism convention in Houston. I had no idea what would come of it when the card came in the mail. In the early 1990s, my job involved a considerable amount of domestic travel and I was happy that I had the membership to accrue the miles. I would go on to join at least

3 more frequent flyer programs during my career.

I am grateful to all of the frequent flyer programs that I have been associated with over the years. The miles that were deposited into my accounts allowed me to travel First Class and Business Class with a companion to Australia, ten times to Europe in Business Class, three times to Asia in Business Class, and to cruise to Alaska in a luxurious suite. There were more trips than these that I just highlighted and I think you get the point and why I am grateful for these programs.

My frequent flyer program accounts would balloon from time to time with all of the global travel and as a result of these massive balances, I was able to gift others with trips. This filled my heart with joy to know that I was giving others the opportunity to create experiences and memories that would last a lifetime.

The miles I gifted to others allowed a family of 4 to travel to the USA for a holiday, a friend to travel to South America to be with her close friends for her birthday, a best friend to travel to New Mexico to share some last moments with a terminally ill mutual friend, and some very close friends to move to South America.

I shared these stories because they showed me what is possible when I have an open mind and a loving heart.

Up, up, and away into the wild blue yonder!!!

Introduction

The concept for this book came to me during my morning reflections one day. I was shocked that it came to me with such clarity. First I had thoughts about the content of the book which included the stories of my experiences with some of the most amazing flight attendants in the sky. One by one the stories started to fill my mind until I had remembered many of the encounters that I had had with flight attendants all over the world.

Later in the day, I sat at my desk and outlined the book from cover to cover. What the front and back covers would look like when the book was published came to me quickly. The stories made up the chapters in the outline and I was now ready to start writing it. I gave myself an aggressive timeline to have the book published in 30 days.

This book is about sharing my everyday experiences and what I learned from them. The experiences seemed normal and mundane on the surface, yet deep and profound when I opened my mind to everything that was supporting me perfectly.

Some of the people we encounter during our everyday life have a meaningful and significant part to play in our lives. In my case, I am highlighting the flight attendants who have had an impact on my life. I could write stories about the people who work in hotels, or restaurants, or stores, or anywhere else who have also had a positive impact on my life as well.

Some of the stories are bigger than just the lessons learned at 35,000 feet.

It really is all about how much we pay attention to others. Are we open to meeting people and making a connection or are we closed off for reasons only known to ourselves?

I love making my everyday life experiences with others out to be much more than they may appear to any observers. Seeing the wonder of meeting people and connecting with them is the stuff that propels my enthusiasm for life. I can honestly say that I look for the deeper meaning in most all of my encounters with other people. I take the time to reflect on what deeper motives are at play in the experience. I am happy to say that I can usually find some universal lessons that make me grow as a person.

I invite you to read this book on three levels. The first is to enjoy the stories that I have shared with you as entertainment. The second is to receive it as a gift from me to you. The third is to read this book with the expectation that the stories will be positive and supportive and will have you smiling at the end of each chapter.

This book is meant to be a feel good collection of stories that inspire and motivate the readers to think and act in their own ways. Find yourself in these stories and see how you relate to them. We are more alike in our life experiences than we are different. We can remain unique without giving up anything about ourselves.

I wish you a pleasant and reflective journey as you read this book. The experience will be yours and yours alone and you will get out of it what is most meaningful to you. Enjoy the trip by being present with this book while you read it. Allow yourself to arrive at a destination that you did not choose before you boarded.

The airport codes are referenced for fun and giggles.

Welcome aboard, ladies and gentlemen. Sit back and relax and enjoy reading these stories of Lessons Learned at 35,000 Feet.

Chapter 1

<u>What I learned about Relationships-1B</u>

At the end of every business trip is the journey home. I loved what I called *going home day* when I was on a business trip. It was the best day of the trip as far as I was concerned. I looked forward to traveling home every time. However, I was sometimes not excited about the actual trip home, especially when it meant long flights, short connections, and multiple time zones.

I am the guy who watches his frequent flyer accounts as if they were bank accounts. After all, you can put a monetary value on the miles you have in your account. I had flown with this airline often over the years and all of my loyalty was about to pay off. In the spring of 2013, I was 54 years old. When I checked in for my flight to start my business trip from SAT-IAH-LHR, I noticed my lifetime miles balance was nearly a million. I knew it would be a momentous achievement when I hit the Lifetime One Million Mile status.

I started to research the benefits that would be bestowed upon me when I hit the Lifetime One Million Miles milestone. The more I found out about the perks, the more excited I got about achieving this status. As usual, I had put the cart before the horse in my excitement and did not calculate the miles needed to hit the million mile marker.

I calculated the miles that I would accumulate from this trip and was certain it was going to be the trip that put me over one million miles. More specifically, the flight from LHR-IAH would be the flight that would give me enough miles to reach one million miles flown during my lifetime. I made a big deal of it in my head and was really more excited about finishing my work week and making my way to the airport.

I normally arrived at the gate early enough to see the flight crew arrive. I started doing this years ago when I was flying the same routes each week with some of the same flight attendants. On this day, I stayed in the lounge longer than normal so I could make the most of every minute of my one million miles flown memories. By the time I arrived at the gate, the flight crew had already boarded the airplane.

I was thrilled that my one million mile flight would be on the Boeing 787 airplane, which had not been in service for very long at that time. I had already flown on it enough times to know that it was going to be an easy flight for me and my body. The technology incorporated into that plane was focused on the passenger's experience and it certainly paid off.

I had always been a traditionalist when it came to commercial aircrafts and my favorite hands down was the Boeing 747. While I will always hold on to the amazing memories I had while flying on the 747, the 787 has won top billing on my list. I will not be side tracked and start in on the Airbus A380.

As they made the announcement for boarding to commence, I was in my usual spot at the front of the line. This was another habit that I picked up while traveling frequently; I made sure I was one of the first to board the plane. It was time to board the plane and I was giddy like it was my first flight. I handed the agent my ticket as she welcomed me to the flight and after she processed it, I walked down the jet way to the airplane.

As I walked towards the airplane door which led into the galley, I saw some of the flight attendants. There were 3 or 4 of them gathered behind the International Services Manager who greeted me as I boarded the airplane. As I made my way into the plane, one of the flight attendants and I recognized each other.

I had flown on several trips with her and we were friends. It was a great surprise to see her and when I reached her, she tackle hugged me. I told her this was my Lifetime One Million Miles flight and that I was thrilled she was on it with me. She was so excited for me and told me that we would catch up when we were up in the air. As I walked towards the aisle and my seat, I heard the man behind me ask the International Services Manager-who is that guy that got the hug. She replied by saying one of our frequent flyers. I felt like a million bucks on my Lifetime One Million Miles flight and we had not even taken off yet.

As I settled into my seat 1B and completed my preflight routine, I was smiling from ear to ear. It was not every day that you were on the flight that brought your lifetime frequent flyer balance to 1 million miles and, as if that was not enough to be excited about, my friend Nancy was on the flight to help me celebrate it. I reflected on the years and trips it took me to get to this milestone as a Road Warrior.

There was something about eating that ice cream sundae on that flight that made it taste just a little more special. Knowing this was the only time I would experience hitting one million lifetime miles with this airline made it memorable. I joined this airline's frequent flyer program in 1987 and about 26 years later, I was a Lifetime One Million Miles frequent flyer. I could not have imagined that this would happen when I first got my card in the mail.

After the dinner service, I made my way to the galley to see if Nancy was there. I found her and we talked for a while and caught up. It was fun to share some time with her. We knew about each other's family and we genuinely cared about each other like real friends. I was very fortunate to have made such a friend from just flying together on several flights over the years which appeared to be such a random experience.

I enjoyed all 10 plus hours of that flight knowing it would be a memory that I would hold on to for a long time. I did not know at the time that I would write about it and share some of the important lessons learned from it. Taking the ordinary and making it extraordinary is a gift that we all have and we can choose to use it whenever we want.

I usually bought my husband a duty-free watch on the flight home, but they did not have the watch I wanted on the cart on this particular flight. Nancy told me to go to the back galley where they had the full inventory and ask if they could find it. I laughed and said that I had not been beyond the curtain in forever and asked her what it was like back there. She laughed and said you can do it. That's what flying upfront will do to you after so many years of it.

I walked past the curtain and made my way through the aisle that was narrower than normal because people were overflowing into it with their arms and legs. I finally made it to the back galley where I found about 5 or 6 flight attendants talking and laughing. I quickly figured out this was the fun place to be.

I asked one of the flight attendants if she could help me find the watch I wanted to buy for 'my husband' and she said that she would be happy to help me. We looked through the carts and she eventually found the watch. After I completed the purchase, I told her and her colleagues that I wanted to stay back here with them for a little while. They told me that I had full run of the plane and that I could stay for as long as I wanted.

We shared stories about where we lived and our lives for about 30 minutes. I then thanked them for making me feel welcomed. I was ready to make my way back to the front of the plane. As I walked up the aisle, I thought to myself, how wonderful it was to be so welcomed by people who were strangers moments earlier. Friendships can last a lifetime or a few minutes, it is all in how we look at them.

I learned that while there are circumstances that bring us together in life, we chose what we do when the circumstances are gone. When I met Nancy for the first time, we had an instant connection. We talked about things that were important to us. We were able to share things about ourselves and become friends quickly.

I remember one time when we were talking in the galley on a flight and I mentioned my partner. She caught me and asked me why I called my husband my partner? I loved that she had brought it to my attention in such a loving and supportive way. We talked about some of my reasons which were rooted in how I thought others might react to my word choice. I realized that my husband was more important to me than any other person and I that I had every right to call him my husband.

Nancy shared her wisdom with me at 35,000 feet, and I discovered that it was also applicable to my life on the ground. I was quick to call him my husband for the rest of our conversation. It was like trying something for the first time and it felt right for me. While I still call him my partner from time to time, I am well aware of it and know the exact meaning when I say it. He is my husband and I use that title because of my friend, Nancy.

When we see the ordinary in our everyday lives as extraordinary, meaningful, and significant; we start to live life more fully and are present with those around us. Those around us can also benefit from how we see friendships and relationships. We create them during the encounters and experiences we have with other people. We make friendships and relationships by feeling loved, valued, and accepted.

Reflections

How do you value your friendships and relationships?

What do you do to show your gratitude for your friends and family being in your life?

How might you take this lesson into your own life?

Chapter 2

What I Learned about Synchronicity-5D

I was 56 in the fall of 2015, when I made yet another business trip. I had already traveled enough times to China to know the ways to make it easiest on me and my body. I knew that the Boeing 787 would provide less jet lag impact on my body, so I made sure that I searched for the flights which included this aircraft when I booked my trip.

Since the majority of the flights to China departed from the West coast, I knew I would layover in LAX or SFO. LAX had the Boeing 787 service and SFO had the 747 service. That made it a tough decision since I loved each aircraft for different reasons. I decided to travel SAT-LAX-PVG-LAX-SAT on this trip.

My flight from SAT-LAX was uneventful and quite routine for me. After so many years of traveling for business, I had adopted some best practices that worked really well for me. One of them was making sure that I had a folder of business reading to take along with me on the flight. I settled into my seat and made the best use of my in-flight time by catching up on some business reading from my folder while listening to my favorite music.

I was always eager and ready to board the airplane and this boarding at LAX was no different. I was among the first in line to board the aircraft and I was ready to get settled into my seat.

I walked onto the plane with a warm welcome from the International Services Manager. I could see the flight attendants in the galley getting things prepared for the flight like I had seen so many times before.

My seat of choice had always been in the bulkhead row. On a recent flight, I talked with the flight attendants about their work assignments on the plane. They shared with me that the last row in the first cabin was the first row of the second service zone. This meant it was just like sitting in the bulkhead row when it came to being served first during the meal service. The advantages of this included a higher chance of getting my first meal choice which was never guaranteed and finishing up and clearing my tray sooner.

The flight attendant came to ask me what I wanted for lunch and I gave her my first choice. Beyond me giving her my order, we started talking about several things that we had in common. The most important thing we had in common was an interest and desire to eat healthy foods. I had been working with a personal fitness trainer for about 6 months by this time and was looking for more ways to eat healthy. She had a lot to share with me in a few minutes and said we could talk more in-flight. I thought how wonderful it was that the flight attendant was interested in healthy eating habits as well as sharing her suggestions with me.

After the meal service was completed and the flight attendants had cleaned up the galley, I went to talk with my new friend, Eloise. We started talking and didn't stop until it was time for her break. When I found out she was a medical doctor who specialized in eastern healing practices, it all started to make sense to me. The more I talked with her, the more I understood about limiting certain foods in my diet. She had a vast set of knowledge that she shared with me about how to eat, when to eat, and how to exercise properly with my trainer and on my own. I was having a consultation with the doctor at 35,000 feet.

We exchanged contact information along with the suggestions that she shared with me for staying on the healthy track. I went to my seat while she went on break and I reflected on what had just happened. With all of the flights that I had taken over the years, I had never met a flight attendant who was a doctor. How things had lined up to put me in that seat on that flight with her as my flight attendant was mind boggling. I wondered if it really was a coincidence that we met in this way or if it was synchronicity.

The flight was coming to an end soon and Eloise came by to talk with me one last time. She asked me to stay in touch and let her know how things went with the suggestions she had written out for me. She also told me to be sure to rest and exercise while in China. As we said our goodbyes, she told me that she hoped that she would see me again on a future flight. I told her that I hoped for the same thing. She did tell me that she was based in SFO and had only taken this flight at the last minute to cover for a friend. I said I might go through SFO in the future and that I would let her know ahead of time to see if we could meet up again.

I thanked her for everything that she had shared with me and told her that she had made a difference by sharing her suggestions. We shared a brief hug before she went to her jump seat for landing.

I used my downtime on this trip to China in some new and different ways. Since I woke up early no matter where I was in the world, I went to the hotel gym each morning. I walked the treadmill and did some weights each morning. Sometimes, I would go back in the evening and walk the treadmill a second time in the same day. I was as committed to my exercising routine as I was to my eating more healthy foods.

After about two weeks in the Chinese countryside for work, it was time to make my way back to Shanghai. I would typically spend a night there before flying home; I decompressed from the work schedule and prepared for the long trip home on my last night in Shanghai.

I booked my flights and hotels well in advance to make sure that I got exactly what I wanted in terms of flight schedules and hotel locations. When I went on the website for the hotel that I had stayed at in Shanghai on all of my previous trips, it was fully booked.

I was glad that I knew Shanghai well enough that I could navigate finding a suitable alternate hotel. While I would normally stay away from a USA based hotel chain while overseas, I found myself looking at one that was in a perfect location in central Shanghai. I went ahead and booked the room despite preferring a Chinese style hotel.

When I arrived at the hotel lobby in Shanghai, it was massive and impressive. It was also overcrowded with western business travelers. I was greeted and checked in with the usual Chinese hospitality, yet with an American flair this time. I was ready to get to my room and settle in before spending some time in the gym on the treadmill.

While I was on the treadmill, I had my earbuds on so I could listen to my favorite music. There were only a few people coming and going during my 45 minute walk. When I went to work out with the weights, there were some new people in the gym. I overheard them talking about their flight schedule. I kept my earbuds off and listened to them long enough to know that they were part of a flight crew from the airline I was flying on the following day. I found it humorous that I was in the same hotel as a flight crew.

My next thought caught me off guard. I found myself wondering if Eloise was there in the hotel and if she would be on the flight to LAX tomorrow. When I finished with my workout, I returned to my room. I picked up my phone and sent a message to Eloise asking her if she was by chance in Shanghai and if she was on the PVG-LAX flight the following day. It was not long before my phone chimed and it was a reply from Eloise.

She was in Shanghai, but in another hotel. She wrote me that the airline had not completed its merger between the flight attendant unions yet and as a result of this situation, the flight crews had to stay at separate hotels. She told me she was in fact on the PVG-LAX flight the next day and she confirmed she would be in the same zone as our previous flight, so she would be my flight attendant again.

After we finished our chat and I sat there reflecting on what had just happened, I was astonished!!! It was one thing to meet her on the flight over and have a connection about my focus on eating healthy; it was another thing altogether to be on the return flight together as well. This was especially baffling since she was not based in LAX.

When I arrived at the gate for my flight, I was smiling from ear to ear. I knew Eloise would arrive soon and I would get to see her on the flight. It felt good to have a friend close by even though I was so far from home. I saw the flight crew walk up to the gate and Eloise looked over and saw me standing in line. She came over and talked with me for a minute before she went on the plane with her colleagues.

When I boarded the plane, it felt surreal knowing that Eloise was already on board. We told each other that we hoped we would see each other just two weeks earlier and now here we were on another flight together!!! When I tried to figure out the odds of that happening, I got lost in the enormity of it.

We were able to spend more time talking on the flight home and we really got to know each other better. It was so kind of her share so much with me about how to stay on track with my healthy focus. It was like my follow-up consultation at 35,000 feet. I was very grateful for both of our 'coincidental' encounters.

I wondered for quite some time after that experience when I reflected on it, if it was by coincidence or not. I believe firmly that these coincidental and synchronized encounters and experiences are only possible when we are in divine alignment. Based on the odds, it would take for them to take place, I chose to see them as miracles and accept them as gifts and blessings.

Reflections

What coincidences show up in your life?

How is synchronicity a part of your life?

How will you be more present to the coincidences and synchronicities in your life?

Chapter 3

What I Learned about Renewal-1K

In June of 2006 I was 47 and I made the decision to leave my corporate career and take a sabbatical. After nearly 25 years of working and building my career with some very challenging roles and assignments, I thought it might be a good idea to recharge for what I thought would be the continuation of my career. I was excited about the opportunities that I thought would come my way during this time away from the schedules, meetings, politics, and fatigue. I thought that I was open to whatever would come my way and then I realized that I was the kind of man to make things happen rather than sit back and wait for them to come to me.

I had been talking with some close friends about making a group trip to Bali together in September of 2006. Due to many unforeseen circumstances, no one was going to be able to make the trip. As I reflected on the trip going from a group of friends going to no one going, I asked myself if I would ever consider going to Bali on my own. My answer was a resounding yes!!!

I began to plan this trip using all of the online resources available to me for the airfare, the hotels, and the guide. It was going to be my first solo trip and my first trip planned completely on the internet. I was ready to dig in and see what adventures would come my way.

My first challenge was to find the best air fare. My research showed me that it was going to be more cost-effective to fly LAX-DPS roundtrip on a discounted business class ticket along with a separate ticket DFW-LAX coming from my frequent flyer account. I booked the LAX-TPE-DPS flight and was ready to now book the DFW-LAX leg.

The first time I booked it, I was off by a day. I booked the DFW-LAX flight to arrive at 5:00PM on the same date as my LAX-TPE-DPS flight, not realizing that that flight departed at 1:00AM. My LAX-TPE-DPS flight would have already left by the time I arrived. When I stacked my flights and realized my error, I called the airline back and asked if I could rebook it with the new date. The agent was kind enough to make the changes with no additional fees. The airfare was now sorted out.

I went on to research hotels in Bali and decided to stay some of the time in Denpasar at the beach and some time in Ubud in the jungle. I found several discounted hotel websites and decided to work with the one that seemed the most credible. They booked directly with the hotel at a huge discount. I booked a two-floor suite at a beach front resort for less than a room at a hotel down the road from me in McKinney, Texas. It was a chain hotel headquartered in Spain that is well known and respected for their service model. I was satisfied with my decision on the hotel for the Denpasar beach stay.

I wanted to find something in Ubud that would give me a true Balinese experience. I found a hotel on the same website that was going to be prefect. It was set on the top of a mountain behind some rice fields in a rural area outside of Ubud's city center. The photos of the chalet made it look like it was hanging off the mountain side with views across the valley. If it was half as impressive in person, it was going to be breathtaking!!!

I booked it and again it was around $75.00 per night with breakfast included. This hotel was associated with an Asian brand and was well known for their top-tier service and accommodations. I also booked my flights so that I could have an extended layover in Singapore on my way home, so I set out to book that hotel as well. I was on the same website looking for hotels in Singapore when I found a five-star Luxury hotel for about $100.00 a night and since this collection of hotels had been on my bucket list, I booked it immediately.

I had booked my airfare and my hotels, I was

ready to find a guide who could transport me around Bali during my stay. Through a website, I found a man who was just starting out with a guide and transportation business. His name was Wayan, I soon learned that all first-born males in Bali were named Wayan. It would be impossible for you to figure out which one I am talking about. I contacted him by email and we made an agreement for him to meet me when I arrived in Bali.

I was thrilled that I had put together a fantastic solo trip and was ready for my big adventure to begin. The day came for me to fly DFW-LAX and then LAX-TPE-DPS and I was bouncing off the walls with excitement. I made my way to LAX and had enough of a layover to walk around and reflect on all my memories of this massive airport that had at one time intimidated me. I realized how fortunate and lucky I was to be in this place getting ready to go to Bali.

My flight LAX-TPE-DPS had a lengthy layover in TPE and I was able to call home and let my partner at the time know that I had made it that far safely. I walked around the airport and bought some things like a Starbucks thermal tumbler and a magnet to remind me of my layover. It was time to say good bye to Taipei and fly on to DPS. I was ready to be there after already traveling for nearly 22 hours.

The arrival in Bali was late at night and Wayan was there waiting for me when I left the arrivals hall. I was relieved that he whisked me off to the resort quickly. We had a good conversation on the way to the resort despite my jet leg and fatigue. We talked about my plans for my time in Bali and we were on the same page. When I arrived at the resort, I was ready to get checked into my suite and go to bed straight away.

I was greeted with a cool wet towel and a watermelon juice by one of the front desk attendants when I arrived in the tropical lobby. I did a double take when he spoke to me in Spanish, and I replied without missing a beat. I remembered it was a Spanish-owned hotel and smiled at feeling the familiarity. My stay in this hotel was amazing, it included walking on the beach at sunrise, being asked to sit with the people who were conducting a cremation ceremony on the beach, participating in a Balinese cooking class, and getting as many massages as I could schedule on the beach or in the spa. When I left the beach for the jungle, I was in a relaxed state of mind.

My time in the jungle fed my soul and made my ego go crazy. I was in a lush tropical jungle with nothing to do...nothing except enjoy my time. I was greeted in the traditional Balinese way with a cool wet towel and juice in a small open air reception building in the middle of the rice fields. I was escorted to the tram that took me down the side of the mountain to my chalet. I lost my breath when I walked in and saw the level of luxury and elegance perched on the mountainside in this chalet.

My time in Bali came to an end all too quickly. I would now fly DPS-SIN. When I checked in for my flight the agent told me that my flight had been canceled and that the airline had rebooked me on another airline. I was so mellow after taming my ego and awakening my soul, I just went with the flow. I arrived in Singapore and went to the hotel to check in.

I arrived at the hotel only to be in culture shock with all of the opulence and luxury that came with this brand. I noticed the increased security that involved my bags being taken from me for scanning while I went though a screening device and hand pat down. When I arrived at the reception desk, I asked the concierge if this was their normal level of security and he replied no; the International Monetary Fund attendees warranted this level of security. I had managed to book the only non-member IMF room in this hotel. I felt very safe in an already secure place. My bags eventually made their way to my room and I was ready to get out and explore some of the sights. My brief time in Singapore allowed me, to visit some of the iconic sights and temples. It was a great place for my re-entry into the real world; I was ready to head back to the USA.

I arrived at the SIN airport and was greeted at the car by an agent who would then walk me though the check-in process and take me to the lounge. I was already impressed with this airline from my short DPS-SIN flight and this seemed way over the top. The check in process was efficient and the lounge was spectacular. I did take time to check out the orchid garden in the airport before boarding the flight SIN-LAX. I love orchids and this was an amazing experience to see so many varieties in one place.

The boarding process was warm, friendly and inviting. I noticed that all of the flight attendants were smiling non-stop. They seemed joyful. I was escorted to my seat by one of the flight attendants and she stayed with me until I was settled in comfortably. I was in seat 1K on the window bulkhead. The aisle seat next to me remained open until the door closed. I was going to have one seat to eat in and another one to look out the window or rest-I had had this happen enough times to know how special it was to be able to spread out into two seats. I was ready to make the very long SIN-LAX trip.

After the meal service was completed, the flight attendant asked me if everything was satisfactory. I replied to her that my expectations had been exceeded. She then asked me a question, that to this day still knocks me for a loop.

She said, "Mr. Bohlender, would you like me to sit next to you and talk with you for little while?"

Being that I am a high extrovert and that I had basically been in silence while I was in Bali, I quickly said yes.

She sat next to me for the next 45 minutes and asked me all about my time in Singapore and Bali. We had a lovely conversation and she was genuinely interested in the stories I shared with her. It was a first for me and I was beyond impressed with that level of caring and kindness.

My entire trip to Bali could be summed up with the words caring and kindness, I was not surprised as I reflected on it that my experience at 35,000 feet would pull it all together. The Balinese people who I met in Denpasar and Ubud were delightfully caring and kind. They had an open-hearted spirit that showed up in every encounter; the kindness of a stranger who saw me walking along the street in Ubud and offered me a ride on the back of his motorcycle to the concert venue that I was walking to, the caring way the family and friends at the cremation ceremony asked me to join them on the beach in Denpasar and above all else Wayan. We shared some great conversations about our mutual appreciation for the music of Jack Johnson and Jimmy Buffet. It was beautiful to see so much caring and kindness in one place.

Reflections

How are you caring and kind to other people?

How do you recognize when others are being caring and kind to you?

How can you be more caring and kind with others in your life?

Chapter 4

What I Learned about Generosity-4B

In the fall of 2006, Janet, the leader of a foundation that helped children attend school in Kenya, which I supported with my contributions, sent me an email reminding me about my upcoming donation for the annual tuition. She was doing some amazing work with these children who were orphaned as a result of the AIDS epidemic. These children did not have a place to live and could not afford the compulsory tuition to attend school. The foundation was focused on providing both housing and education to these orphans.

Janet traveled from her home in the USA to Kenya two times each year and stayed for months at a time. The purpose of her extended trips was to ensure that the work of the foundation was being completed appropriately. She also invited donors to join her on the trips for an opportunity to do service work, meet the children and explore parts of Kenya. I had entertained the idea to go on one of these trips ever since I started my relationship with the foundation in 2000.

Janet's email was like all of the previous ones giving me some information about the children's progress with their studies and the foundation's activities and achievements in Kenya. As we exchanged emails like text messages back and forth quickly that morning, it occurred to me to ask about the upcoming trips to Kenya for 2007.

I asked Janet if she had any space available for me to join her and a group on a trip. She replied to me that she was inviting a small group in February, and asked if that was something I would be interested in doing. When I found out it would be Janet, her sister, her long time best friend, and a married couple; I jumped at the chance and said yes.

I liked the idea of being part of an intimate group visiting with the children and doing our service work together. In less than 10 minutes and 6 emails, I was confirmed for a trip to Kenya in February 2007. The fun part would start after it sank in that I was going to Kenya in less than 6 months. Janet let me know that everything while I was in country would be covered by her planning contact. My only next step for me was to book the airfare and any layovers I wanted to have along the way.

I began to search for airfares by first looking at my frequent flyer account. I was ecstatic that I had more than enough miles in my balance to redeem them for a roundtrip business class ticket DFW-NBO roundtrip!!! I called the airline and booked the flights.

My first flight was DFW-IAH-LHR with a 6-hour layover in London. I was very excited about this layover knowing it would give me enough time to get into central London and see some of my favorite spots, including a cafe for breakfast near Trafalgar Square.

The second leg of the trip would be LHR-ZHR and the connection required an overnight stay. When I booked it, I was thrilled about the chance to spend some time in Zurich!!! I had a weekend layover there years before and really enjoyed the city.

My final flight to Kenya was ZUR-NBO which would leave in the morning and arrive late in the evening on the same day. It would be my first time flying over the Mediterranean Sea and the Sahara Desert which I was quite excited about!!!

My return flights would be less arduous NBO-LHR-IAH-DFW, all without any extended connections or layovers. After several weeks in Kenya, I had the feeling that I would be ready to be at home.

I arrived at the Zurich airport earlier than required for my flight because I was anxious about my 3 checked bags. When I left DFW, the agent told me that with my flight break in ZUR, I would be governed by that airline's baggage allowance. He explained that the 3 bags I checked in Dallas would be limited to 2 bags and there would likely be an excess baggage fee. The moment of truth arrived and

I told my story to the front counter agent in ZUR about the 3rd bag. I explained to her that it was filled with school supplies and hygiene products for the Kenyan children who I was going to visit in the orphanages and schools.

She calmly and professionally told me that the excess baggage fee was the equivalent of about $2000.00 USD. I told her that I was not prepared to pay that amount for the bag and asked if there were any other options. She told me that the only other option for getting it there was to send it freight with a forwarder company and that they had a kiosk on the other side of the airport. I finished my check-in process and went to the kiosk.

I showed up at the kiosk with the bag and explained my situation. The agent understood and explained my options for getting the bag to NBO. I chose the option that was quoted which was the equivalent of about $800.00 USD. And, before I could reply to the quote, the agent said I would only be charged the equivalent of $600.00 USD because I was doing humanitarian work in Kenya. I thanked the agent and paid the fee before I left for the lounge. I was told the bag would arrive in NBO in about 10 days.

While I was in the lounge, I was thinking about how grateful I was that it had all been sorted. I was ready to enjoy the flight to NBO. I was appreciative of the agent's generosity in quoting me a reduced fee for the bag to get to NBO. All in all, I was in a good frame of mind with all of that behind me.

I was excited to finally board the airplane and get settled into my seat, 4B. It was the last row in the cabin which was a new thing for me because I usually sat in the bulkhead. The flight attendants came by my seat and welcomed me warmly with their Swiss style of hospitality. They were precise, professional, and polite.

The flight was filled with lots of things to enjoy. I was able to look out the window and see us flying over Italy ending up at the end of the boot over the Mediterranean Sea. It was an amazing view!!! We reached Africa and then I could see the Sahara Desert below. It seemed like we had been flying over it for a long time, giving me the sense of how massive it must be. During the flight we were served a breakfast and later on a lunch.

The flight attendants came out with the carts, one after the other, for the breakfast service and each cart was filled with something different. Fruits, yogurts and cereals were on one while pastries and breads were on another. There was also one with the eggs, breakfast meats and sides. It was quite impressive to see the vast range of choices for making my unique breakfast-it rivaled any 5-star brunch experience on the ground.

When the flight attendant arrived at my row with the first cart, she asked the gentleman on the window what he wanted from the trays. She added that he could have anything and everything he wanted and as much as he wanted. When she asked me what I wanted, I asked her if the same applied to me. She smiled and said, of course because this was the last row and that there was no limit to what we could enjoy with our meal. Of all places, I had found food heaven at 35,000 feet.

I had the same experience with lunch and enjoyed all of my choices and all of the vast variety of foods I tasted. I was grateful for their hospitality and generosity with not only the meal services but also the overall inflight experience.

I landed in NBO late in the evening and was fatigued from the long journey. When I met Janet and her Kenyan driver, Maurice, I was emotionally and physically drained and desperately needed a hug. I asked Janet if she was a hugger and she replied yes, so we hugged. It felt good!!! I shook Maurice's hand and as we walked toward the van, Janet whispered to me that the Kenyan culture was very reserved and that it was very rare for Kenyans to hug or hold hands in public. I thanked her for telling me; I made a mental note of it to make sure that I did not offend anyone just by asking-if the occasion came up.

We went to the church service at the orphanage on Sunday morning so we could meet the children and their caregivers. During the service, one little girl who was about 3 years old went from lap to lap sitting with many of the caregivers When she spotted the 6 of us with Janet, she began to make her rounds from one lap to another. I was impressed at how brave she was to move from one stranger to the next. Wanda came back and sat with me again for quite a while longer and we had such a wonderful time smiling at each other.

Our service work began on a Monday with painting the inside of the cottages that the children lived in. Each cottage had a family room, dining room, kitchen, 2 bedrooms and a bathroom. There was 1 caregiver parent in the house with as many as 8 children. The concept was to create a family feeling for the children who had lost their whole families. Wanda was the only child in the orphanage since she was too young to attend school. She was playing with her caregiver in the playground in the center of all of the houses. The time for our mid-morning break came quickly.

Being in Kenya and feeling the British influence was apparent when we arrived for our first break. The break area was outdoors and there was a pot of tea and some pastries. It wasn't high tea but it was delicious in every way. When I cleared the dishes and took them to the kitchen window, I could see into the cooking area. I asked the woman what they were making and she invited me in to see for myself.

I went into the kitchen and was introduced to the women who were cooking lunch for the children. There was a massive pot of soup on the burner and next to it was a flat iron grill. There was a woman making flatbread on it. She had the dough in a bowl and would roll out each one before placing them individually on the hot flat iron grill. I was intrigued by this process. I think she could tell and asked me if I wanted to make some. I said yes and started to make some for the children's lunch.

I felt a connection to the children while painting their cottages, making the flatbread and seeing their art work on the walls in the orphanage compound. I was grateful that I could be of service to these children and their caregivers. I knew that they were happy with their lives and were grateful for us being there with them.

The day the bag of school supplies arrived, we spent the entire day with the customs broker processing all of the paperwork to get the bag cleared. It was an all-day affair going from one office to another. As lunch time approached, we were still not finished, so we knew we would have to go back later for the final steps in the process.

The final step was to meet with a customs deputy and make my case with the documents for why this bag should be allowed into Kenya. His office doors were flanked by 2 machine gun-armed guards when I arrived with my customs agent. I was intimidated and at the same time confident about getting those school supplies to the children. After a brief tense conversation, he stamped the paperwork with authority. We now had the bag and we could deliver the supplies to the school at Kibera, the largest slum in Kenya and in the world.

In between completing the service work and the visiting the school at Kibera, we had some rest breaks. We traveled to the Mt. Kenya Safari Club, Lamu Island and the Masai Mara.

My time at the Mt. Kenya Safari club was relaxing and restful. I enjoyed the vintage British atmosphere of the lodge and the grounds. It was a window into Kenya as it was in the 1950s. I made a donation to the animal refuge in my mom's name so she has a tile with her name on it on one of the buildings.

Lamu Island was a new experience for me. It was like no other island I had ever visited. We landed at a grass airstrip on the mainland and took a motorized boat to our resort on the island. We arrived and were greeted by a lovely Kenyan couple whose families had come to Kenya in the 1950s.

Their resort was made up of one main thatched building that served as the reception area, bar, dining room, and lounge. The cement block building behind it was about the size of a one-car garage and it was the kitchen. The thatched cottages were scattered along the Indian Ocean beach with lots of privacy and seclusion because of the sand dunes. It was a breathtaking place.

On my first morning I woke up early and looked out at the beach and saw the low tide. The shoreline was stretched out into the ocean and it invited me to explore it. I went out and walked for what felt like an hour only to realize that I might need to get back to the beach before the tide came back in. It was amazing to see the sea shells and tide pools along with the sea life as I walked back. Until this day, it remains one my top 10 sunrise beach walks anywhere in the world.

The woman who owned the resort with her husband was very gregarious and we got along famously. I mentioned at breakfast that morning that I had enjoyed the dinner the night before, and she asked me if I wanted to join her in the kitchen to prepare dinner that night and of course, I said yes. She was delighted and told me that we would go over to the mainland to a market to fetch some ingredients. I was ready in a flash and off we went in the boat. We made our way through the open market and bought some fruits and vegetables. With our sacks in hand, it was time to return to the resort.

When we arrived on the beach, there was a mesh netted bag filled with shrimp of all sizes floating in the water at the shoreline. She picked it up and said this was part of the dinner menu. Later when I joined her in the kitchen with her team, I was amazed at how welcoming they all were to me. I felt at home. Dinner that night was especially yummy because I helped prepare it. The hospitality of the people on Lamu Island left an everlasting impression on me.

I was a few weeks into my trip, with more service work completed, when it was time to fly to the Masai Mara for our safari. I remember a lot about that trip like the fact that the plane had propellers like a private airplane not a commercial one and my one bag could not weigh more than 22 pounds. The plane would stop and drop off passengers at several lodges along the way and then pick up passengers on the way back; this seemed to be a very efficient use of the one flight a day between WIL-MRE. I also noticed that the baggage handler jumped out of the back of the plane with bags when we landed on the grass airstrip. It truly was an adventure.

The welcome at the safari lodge was warm and sincere, they were genuinely happy to see us. I was struck by the attention to service and detail. After everything was explained to me about my stay with regard to the meals, the safaris and the monkeys; I was ready to go to my tent. However, when I was informed about the monkeys, I was not happy as I have a huge aversion to them.

When I walked into my 'tent' I asked the attendant if this was for real. It was a five-star luxury suite made of canvas. I had a living room and a front deck overlooking a river bend below and a king-sized bedroom with ensuite. I thought I was never going to leave this place. Then I remembered why I was there and quickly went to the meeting place for the first safari.

After the first safari, I was hooked. I wanted to see it all. I wanted to experience everything I could while on the Masai Mara. At dinner that night, I gave my compliments to the server and asked her to share them with the chef. In a matter of minutes, the head chef was at our table and he invited me to join him and his team in the kitchen the next afternoon. He wanted me to see first hand how the meals were prepared. I was overwhelmed with anticipation!!!

The following afternoon when I got back from the safari, I ran to the kitchen. When I arrived, the head chef welcomed me and gave me a chef's jacket, hat and a name plate from the lodge. I quickly put it all on and he walked me around from prepping stations to cooking stations. I met everyone on the team including the pastry chef. I helped her make cashew tarts and a fruit salad for dessert. While I was preparing some of the fruit, the general manager came by and talked with me. He thanked me for recognizing the kitchen team and said it was unprecedented in his tenure. I told him that I thought it was important to say these things to people and that it was ingrained in me as a leader. He asked me if he could take my picture with the pastry chef and I said of course.

At the table that night when dinner was finished, the head chef, pastry chef and general manager all came to our table. They wanted to thank me for my attention and interest in the work that they do at the lodge. The general manager handed me a small bag and asked me to open it. In the bag was a brightly colored Masai style painted picture frame with the photograph of me and the pastry chef in it. I was humbled by their generous gesture and thanked them-with hugs that they readily accepted. This picture frame has been on my home office desk for the past 12 years!!!

My time in Kenya came to end after several weeks and I found myself where I started at NBO late at night with Janet and Maurice. When I got out of the van, I hugged Janet goodbye and thanked her for the experience of a lifetime. When I went to shake Maurice's hands he grabbed me and hugged me tightly. It seemed that all of the time that we had shared, the conversations we had, the visit with his family and the work we had done together made him feel like my brother. He wanted me to know he cared for me and was grateful that he met me.

I was overwhelmed and waited until I was safely in my seat on the airplane before I released my tears. I started to share this story of hospitality and generosity at 35,000 feet and quickly realized that this trip was special. It was all about the human spirit at 35,000 feet and at sea level and at the equator in Kenya. This entire trip punctuated for me the happiness and connection that we feel when we are hospitable and generous with each other.

Reflections

How are you hospitable with you friends and family?

What are some of the ways you are generous with other people?

How can you be more hospitable and generous with other people in your life?

Chapter 5

What I Learned about Compassion-3A

I can say without a doubt that one of the worst experiences of my life was when I traveled while being sick. I am not talking about a cold or headache, I am talking about being really sick with the flu or something that drains your energy and knocks you down hard.

I have traveled sick on several occasions and I can tell you from personal experience that they were some of the worst flights of my life and that included that flight when there was scary turbulence that caused the plane to drop unexpectedly.

I remember one flight MEX-IAH when I started passing kidney stones in flight. I was in the first row bulkhead and the small plane had a lavatory in the aft of the plane. After passing through the aisle 3 or 4 times, I asked the flight attendant if I could sit with her in the exit row. She kept me company and helped take my mind off the pain while we talked.

I look back on that flight now and I realize it was a dress rehearsal for what was to come on the flight PVG-YVR in the fall of 2013. I was at the end of my work trip to China and had just settled in at the hotel for my final night before flying home. I rested and had an easy night in the hotel. Unfortunately when I woke up on 'going home day', I was very ill. I woke up with a bad case of Chairman Mao's revenge. I thought it was very ironic because I had only eaten western style foods the day before. Nonetheless, I had to make a decision about traveling home in this predicament or not.

I decided that I had to get home and stayed with my original travel schedule. I stayed in my hotel room until it was time to go to the airport. My anxiety level rose as I made my way out of the hotel room and to the car that would take me to the hotel. I took a dose of Imodium before I got into the car.

I was able to make the drive to the airport with nothing more than a loud gurgling sound coming from my tummy. I was relieved to get checked in for the flight quickly and then managed to make my way to the lounge. While in the lounge, I started to rethink my decision to fly home with this tummy issue. It was not the first time that I had questioned myself for making the decision to put other things ahead of my own health.

I had a history of putting the other person's oxygen mask on and then neglecting to put my own on. It was a bad habit that I hoped someday to break. Sadly that day was not today. I was already checked in and sitting in the lounge when it occurred to me that I had made a questionable decision.

It came time for me to go to the gate and to board the airplane. I was in the line waiting for the boarding process to start when I realized that I needed to visit the restroom before I boarded the airplane. I gave up my place in line and for me that was a big deal.

By the time I returned to the boarding line, almost everyone had already boarded the airplane. I was able to walk on the airplane and go directly to my seat rather quickly.

I was flying on a different airline from my regular one for the first time so it took me a minute to settle in and get my bearings. I was in seat 3A which meant I had a short walk to the lavatory. I kept telling myself that I could make this 11-hour flight without incident.

One of the many lessons that I keep learning over and over is asking for help from others. There was a time when I was so fiercely independent that I did not even know how to form the sentence for asking for help. I could not imagine asking anyone for help and as a result I did not do it very often. I already had many life experiences that showed me that I could do it on my own. I completed my university studies and earned my degree on my own. The only exception being the tuition reimbursement program that I participated in with my company. If I could do all that on my own, I could do anything on my own.

My need to be independent was challenged once again. While we were still at the gate, I went to talk with the flight attendant. I spoke with her discreetly about my condition and let her know that I may need to get to the lavatory more frequently than normal or while the seat belt sign was illuminated.

When I told her about my case of Chairman Mao's revenge she laughed and then she offered some genuine support. She asked me if I wanted her to make a seat swap so I could be closer to the lavatory. I told her that that was very kind of her and that I preferred to not bring any additional attention to myself. She understood and said that I didn't need permission to do what I thought would be best for me while in flight keeping in mind my own safety.

As I got ready to return to my seat, she told me everything would be okay and that she was there to take care of me. I was very grateful for her concern and compassion and felt relaxed knowing I had someone watching out for me.

Once we were in the air, the flight attendants started the meal service. I had already decided that I was not going to eat anything because I could not take the risk of making the condition worse. When the flight attendant came to my seat, she asked me what I wanted to eat. I told her that I thought it would be better to forgo eating anything. She said she understood and offered me a soda that might aid in settling my tummy. I took the drink from her and drank it very slowly, I realized it was indeed calming my tummy.

I felt my tummy relaxing after a couple of the sodas and got excited about getting something to eat. The flight attendants were finished with the meal serve by this time so I walked up to the galley to talk with my flight attendant. I told her that I thought the soda had helped calm my tummy and asked her if there was something I could try to eat. We agreed that the cheese plate might be a good option. I went back to my seat and waited for her to bring me the cheese plate.

I think I ate that cheese plate at the slowest pace I had ever eaten anything in my life. I was very methodical about taking a piece of cheese and savoring it while I ate it. It was like eating my first meal ever and I enjoyed it, a lot. When I finished eating the cheese plate, the flight attendant came by and picked up the dishes. She asked me how I was feeling and I told her that I was feeling a lot better now.

The combination of the Imodium, the sodas, the cheese plate and the compassionate care from my flight attendant all made me feel better. I was relieved that I was feeling better with about half of the flight left. Now I hoped to enjoy watching a movie.

When we landed and we were making our way to the gate, the flight attendant came over to my seat to talk with me. She told me that she was glad that I had recovered some of my health on the flight and wished me a safe onward journey. I told her that her unique brand of concern and compassion had helped me feel better and I was very grateful to her for being there for me. I had made yet another flight attendant friend.

When the airplane arrived at the gate and the door opened, I made my way off the plane with one last thank you for my flight attendant who was standing at the galley opening. She was my caregiver at 35,000 feet.

Reflections

How do you show others your compassion for them?

What are some ways you are compassionate with others?

What will do you differently in showing your compassion for others now?

Chapter 6

<u>What I Learned about Perfection-9K and 2L</u>

I woke up very early for my flights LHR-IAH-SAT in the spring of 2013, I was ready to be home again after another work trip to the UK. I made my way to the lifts on my floor in the hotel and when I got there, I noticed this other guest standing there waiting for a lift to come to our floor. When I saw him, I instantly thought that he was an air marshal just by his appearance. We were on the same shuttle to the airport and went to the same terminal.

I went to the counter and got checked in quickly. I made my way through the security like I had done so many times in the past. After I finished my snack and coffee in the lounge, I made my way to the shopping area for one last look around before boarding the flight. I bought some tea and other gifts so now I was ready to go to my gate.

The boarding process becomes all too familiar when you have done it as many times as I have already, yet I thought this one was going to be an exception. I saw the man from the hotel lifts from earlier that morning standing at the gate with 3 other men. They were all dressed in a similar way with pressed jeans and polo shirts. They all had a similar short cropped haircut and were wearing steel-toe boots. I am very observant when I travel and I now had it figured out that they were all air marshals.

Before the announcement to board was made, all 4 of them disappeared. I wondered where they went and then figured it out or so I thought. There was another flight to the USA at the gate next to ours and I thought that 2 went on that flight while the other two were on my flight. I thought that they had to go on before any of the passengers and get their gun cases. I finished the story in my head and boarded the airplane.

I walked onto the airplane and passed through the galley to get to my seat 9K. When the flight attendant came to my seat, we hit it off right away. She had a bubbly and engaging personality. I thought to myself, we are going to have a great flight together!!!

Everything was perfect until it came time for the meal service. I was enjoying my meal and realized that I needed to visit the lavatory. I had never gotten up mid-meal before so this would be a new thing for me. I folded the tray in half and left it standing up while I got out of my seat. I went to the lavatory and came back to my seat to finish my meal.

When the meal service was finished and the flight attendant came to clear my tray, we realized that I had broken it. The tray linen was caught in the tray in such a way that it could not be removed. I was upset with myself for doing such a dumb thing, but the flight attendant was kind and considerate about it. The flight attendant brought the International Services Manager and a male colleague to my seat to try to fix it. We laughed while they tried their best to extract the table linen from the tray and it would not come out. I was told that I could not sit in the seat for landing for safety reasons and that I would have to move to another seat. I was embarrassed by this point.

When the ISM came back to my seat to tell me where my new seats was located, I was surprised to find out that I would be going up to first class to sit in the cockpit crew rest seat. I asked when I needed to move and she told me that she would come and get me when their final break was over. I waited eagerly for her to come back and get me.

When she came to get me, I gathered my stuff and followed her to the new seat 2L. The flight attendant in first class welcomed me to her cabin and laughed when she told me she had heard that I had broken a part of the plane. As I settled in for the remainder of the flight, I looked over at the seats across from me and saw, you guessed it, the 2 men who I thought were air marshals. Now I knew I was right with the story I had made up about them.

The final piece of evidence was revealed when we landed and they were getting ready to leave the airplane. They both had these small cases with them that looked something like what you might find a drill or other hand tool in with them as they left the airplane. These were the gun cases that I imagined they had to go and get before boarding the airplane. It felt good to be right about something after I had broken the tray table.

I am the model first born child which includes my drive to be prefect and do things the right way. When I broke the tray table, it caused me to reflect on my need to be perfect. I learned once again that perfection is an illusion and an unattainable goal. While being the best I could be is within my control, being perfect is illusive and outside of my grasp. I can now laugh and share this story in all of its perfect imperfection.

<u>Reflections</u>

How are you imperfect?

How do you make peace with being imperfect?

How will you show up imperfectly now?

Chapter 7

What I Learned about Luck-21C

In the early part of the 1990s, my job required me to commute to several other cities on a regular basis. I was officially a Domestic Road Warrior with most of my time spent away from home. I thrived on this experience and made sure I learned the most that I could from it. While it was sometimes a grueling and hectic schedule, there were times that I could to step back and have some downtime.

I remember working in Jacksonville during one week in particular. I finished my week and went to the airport on Friday afternoon to make my way home. I say home, but what I really mean to say is that I was flying to Houston to meet up with my partner at the time and some of our best friends. We were all going to Las Vegas for the weekend and I was only stopping in Houston to meet up with them for the next flight to Lost Wages.

When I arrived in Houston, they were already waiting for me at my arrival gate. It was nice to be met by all of them when I got off the airplane. We were all excited about going to Las Vegas for the weekend. Why 5 grown men were so excited about the idea of going to Lost Wages and gambling away their hard earned money was funny to me. I was not much of a gambler, I would really only put into the slot machines what money I was willing to pay for entertainment.

As a road warrior, I was almost always upgraded to first class and I enjoyed the bigger seats with more leg room, the amenities and the snack and meal services. My flight from JAX-IAH was in first class and now I was going to board this flight with my friends to LAS in coach. I was; however, looking forward to this flight knowing we would have fun anywhere as long as we were all together.

I sat in 21C next to my best friend, Edward, who was in the middle seat. Taking the middle seat was a clear sign of a best friend, after all I had made the ultimate sacrifice to sit in coach with him. We were settled in and started laughing at the banter that we shared with each other. It was fun to relax and be on a flight that was taking me to a vacation and not to work. This was going to be a fun weekend.

At some point during the flight, the flight attendant made an announcement. She told us that there was going to be a drawing to get us all ready for Las Vegas. She went on to share with us that one lucky passenger would be taking some cash off the airplane with them. That got our attention!!! We stopped laughing long enough to listen to the instructions.

The flight attendant announced that anyone who wanted to participate would need to have a single dollar bill. She told us to write our seat number on the dollar bill. After we had time to do that, the flight attendant came through the aisle with a plastic bag to collect all of the dollar bills in it. When all of the dollar bills had been put in the bag, she pulled one out and the passenger whose seat number was written on it would win the bag of cash. It seemed very straightforward and risk free to play for only a single dollar.

I told Edward that we should do it. He told me that he did not have a dollar bill in his wallet. I reached for my wallet and when I opened it, there were two one dollar bills in it. I gave him one and I wrote 21C on the other one. We got all excited at the idea of winning the bag of cash!!!

The flight attendant came by and I dropped our dollar bills into the bag. She said good luck and I said thank you. She made her way to the front of the airplane with the bag which was now filled with cash. I was in an aisle seat so I leaned over to see the front of the airplane where the flight attendant was holding the bag of cash. I could see her from all the way back there.

She made an announcement that she was ready to pull the lucky dollar bill. As she pulled out the dollar bill and turned it to read the seat number on it, I said to Edward. "That's my dollar bill". I won the bag of cash. He laughed and we waited to hear her announce the winning seat number.

She announced that the winning seat was 21C. That was indeed my seat. Edward laughed and said something like you lucky s*$t, while others on the plane groaned loudly.

I watched the flight attendant make her way to my seat and when she got to me she congratulated me on winning the bag of cash. I thanked her for the bag as she handed it to me. Edward was quiet now with the cash bag on my tray table. He then said let's count it and see how much you won. As he counted it, I was jumping in my seat with anticipation and excitement about how much money was in the bag.

He had worked in a bank while in college and was very skilled at taking this mess of dollar bills out of the plastic bag and starting to organize them. I have intense OCD when it comes to putting cash in order and it was too overwhelming to me to have this disorganized pile of dollar bills in front of me.

Edward began to quickly sort the dollar bills and before I knew it, he had lots of stacks of the dollar bills on both of our tray tables. Each stack contained 10 bills or $10. He then picked up each one counting it by 10 and when he finished, there was $78 in cash. I was so excited that I had turned my $2, one for me and one for Edward, into $78. I was ready for Las Vegas now that I had already had a winning streak at 35,000 feet.

I learned on that flight that being fortunate and lucky was only possible if you were willing to play the game. If I wanted to find out if I was lucky or not, I had to take the chance. Fortune and luck can only show up if you have put something into the game.

It is interesting to me that as I reflect on this story, that I only had 2 single dollar bills in my wallet. I had just enough for me and Edward. I did not think twice about giving him the extra dollar bill, it came naturally to me to give to others.

I am grateful for my intuition that told me that it was my dollar bill even before the announcement was made. I have relied on my intuition a lot during my life and I can see how trusting my gut has rewarded me in both my personal and professional life. Yet, sometimes people see the outcomes as being fortunate or lucky.

I am the kind of risk-taker who quickly assesses the data he has in front of him and makes a decision. It appears to be impulsive to some because I can make decisions rather quickly when I have enough of the information I think I need to decide on something. My mind works rapidly when processing information that leads to a decision.

My decision to play the bag of cash game may have looked spontaneous to others because I jumped at the chance to play before she even finished the full announcement, but in addition to being a risk taker, I enjoy healthy competition. In this case it was me against the other passengers on the airplane.

I learned that being fortunate and lucky might put some others off since not everyone loves a winner. While my best friend, Edward, was excited for me, there were 76 other passengers who were not. It comes with the territory that others will have negative reactions and feelings about your luck. It is important not to let them steal your joy or celebration in winning.

People who cannot see themselves as fortunate or lucky will likely get their wish. How can you be fortunate or lucky if you begrudge it for others? There is a responsibility that comes with being fortunate and lucky, and it includes being kind and considerate to others. I find encouraging others to believe it can happen for them diffuses the negativity.

It is important to understand how our mindset plays out in whether we think we are deserving of fortune and luck. If you think you will win, you may very well win. If you think you will lose, you may very well lose. Given the choices that you have, which would you prefer to experience? When we are excited about winning, we are able to accept our right to be fortunate and lucky.

I went to Las Vegas a few more times after that original trip and I don't remember the bag of cash game on that same airline or the other airlines that I flew. What I do know is that I was fortunate and lucky on that flight on the Friday night flying to Las Vegas. And what I learned from that is that if I can have that experience at 35,000 feet, I can have it on the ground as well.

I left Las Vegas with the net cost of the trip being less than $100.00 a day. My airfare, hotel, meals, entertainment and gambling costs against my winnings left me with a balance of $300.00 for 3 days. I felt very fortunate and lucky to have had such an amazing opportunity to learn more about the value and importance of being fortunate and lucky.

Reflections

How does being fortunate and lucky show up in your life?

Do you see the impact of being fortunate and lucky on your life?

What would you do differently if you believed your were fortunate and lucky?

Chapter 8

What I Learned about Dreams-2K

I was 28 years old in 1987 when I signed up for my frequent flyer program when I attended a travel expo. It was an exciting time for me to walk the convention center floor with all of the travel booths. I filled my tote with brochures and pamphlets from almost every booth. My favorite take away was my temporary frequent flyer member card.

I had no idea that when I signed up for that frequent flyer program what a big deal it would be in my life. I made the decision that I would only fly this airline so that I could accumulate enough miles to redeem them for a free trip someday!!!

My frequent card collected more dust than miles for the first few years and then in the early 1990s, I started to travel for my job. My job gave me the opportunity to travel every week and before too long I saw my frequent flyer account balance start to rise.

As my frequent flyer account balance increased, I decided it was time to get serious about how I might redeem the miles for a free trip. After all, that was my dream when I signed up for the program-free travel. I had a brochure that showed me every possible redemption option for my miles.

I spent hours looking through the brochure and was most interested in the international destinations and the required miles for a round trip. I was most excited about redeeming the miles for a trip to Australia so that is where I focused all of my attention.

I have always been driven to achieve my goals and this situation was not going to be any different. When I looked at my balance on my frequent flyer account and what it would take to travel to various international destinations, I knew I had my work cut out for me to close the gap. I decided that I would to go for the big trip to Australia.

I looked at the miles required for a roundtrip ticket IAH-SYD and saw that it was 75,000 miles per person in economy. I thought to myself that it would take a lot to get all the way up to 150,000 miles for me and my partner at the time to make the trip. I set my intentions on earning enough miles to redeem them for those award tickets. What followed after I made that decision is still crazy when I think about it. I watched my frequent flyer account balance grow with every trip I took. And when there were contests to earn bonus miles with the airlines or partner hotels, I signed up every time. I was amazed at how quickly the balance was increasing.

I looked at my account balance one day, a couple of years after I started traveling for work and saw that I was almost at the 150,000 miles balance required for the 2 roundtrip economy tickets IAH-SYD. When I saw the progress that I had made, I decided that it was time to set a new intention for the award trip to Australia.

I reviewed the award chart and saw that 2 roundtrip business class tickets IAH-SYD would require 100,000 miles per person. I got very excited about the idea of traveling to Australia in business class and decided that it was going to be my new intention. I was ready to rack up the miles and redeem them for a trip of a lifetime.

In a matter of a year or so, I had accumulated enough miles in my frequent flyer account to have a balance close to 200,000 miles. This was about the time that I was attending classes to complete my BA degree and I knew that there was no way that we could make that kind of a trip at this time. I thought it might be a great graduation gift to travel to Australia and I decided that the trip would take place in July 1996. As 1995 was coming to an end and I looked at my account balance, I saw that it had grown to almost 250,000 miles. I went back to the awards chart one more time!!!

There on the award chart as big and bold as it could be was the award for 1 roundtrip first class ticket IAH-SYD at 125,000 miles per person. I knew this was what all of the traveling was leading up to and got very excited about the idea of flying first class to Australia. When I had a balance in my frequent flyer account of over 250,000 miles in early 1996, I booked the trip for July of that same year.

I remember thinking that the flight from LAX-SYD was going to be the longest flight I had taken so far. It seemed like a dream would come true to me. I was excited about traveling to my 4th continent. I remember boarding the Boeing 747 in LAX and going to our seats 2KL near the nose. It was great to be on board my dream plane going to my dream destination. The flight attendant who welcomed us on board was very attentive from the very first encounter. I could tell that she was a consummate professional flight attendant.

During the flight, we had some of the best service ever which was, in some cases way over the top. The flight attendant was able to anticipate our every want or need and be there with it before we could say anything to her. She was professional, polite, and polished. I could tell that she was working with a different standard than many of the flight attendants I had flown with up until then.

I spent some time talking with her by the bar area while in flight and learned a lot about her career and the airline. In addition to being one of the safest airlines in the world, it also had an impeccable reputation for its long haul service. I was delighted to experience both on this flight. She explained to me that all of the flight attendants who flew in first class had to make a special application for it. In addition to applying for it, when they were accepted into the elite first class flight attendant cadre, they would have to complete an extensive training program focused on the service levels that they would deliver to the passengers.

This investment in the flight attendants was visible in the service that we received in flight. The flight had a brief stop in AKL where all but 4 of us left the first class cabin. These open seats would become important to me as we began our approach into SYD.

The flight attendant came by our seats at the end of the flight and gave us some thank you gifts-a bottle of Australian wine and a CD with Opera music from the Sydney Opera House. I was impressed with receiving these gifts and thanked the flight attendant. She told me that it was her pleasure to serve me on this flight. She went on to tell me that I had a very effervescent personality. It was the first time anyone said that to me and I felt like a million bucks!!!

The last act of hospitality came when 2 of the flight attendants came to get us and move us to the left side of the plane. They told us that it was the side of the plane that you could see the approach over the harbor. I sat in the window seat with the flight attendant sitting next to me pointing out the beaches, the city center and the bridge. It was spectacular to see for the first time!!!

The trip to Australia was a massive success and we enjoyed visiting several cities around the country-Sydney, Brisbane, Melbourne, and Cairns. One of my favorite parts was seeing our friends who we met while on vacation in Europe during the summer of 1993. They had extended an invitation to us to visit them in Australia and we showed up!!!

When the time came to fly home, I reflected on the dream trip. It was a trip of a lifetime. I was very grateful for experiences and knew that I would think about it for years to come. I loved that my dream came true!!!

I went on to continue to travel for work and vacation all the while depositing miles into my frequent flyer account. By early 2002, I had racked up a balance close to 200,000 miles again. I knew exactly what I wanted to redeem those miles for on the award chart. Without hesitation I knew that I was going to book 2 round-trip business class tickets with the outbound trip SAT-IAH-PHX-LAX-SYD-BNE and the return trip SYD-AKL-LAX-IAH-SAT.

In December 2002, my partner at the time and I made our way to Australia for an exciting vacation down under. It was not lost on me that I was going back to Australia for a second dream vacation. And the part that still stuns me to this day is that both trips were made redeeming miles which meant that I only paid the taxes for each trip.

This story is less about the lessons learned at 35,000 feet and more about the stories that led up to the flights that took me to Australia and New Zealand two times in less than 10 years. The important lesson for me with both of these trips was setting the intentions and goals and then going after them. By focusing on the work needed to achieve my intentions and goals, I was able to experience 2 dream trips down under!!!

Reflections

How do your intentions motivate you?

What are some of your dreams?

How will go after your intentions and dreams now?

Chapter 9

What I Learned about Surprises-1B

I made plans to travel to India to visit a friend and former colleague in August 2010. I was going to make the trip from China since I had to be there for work. I looked into the airfares and shopped for the best deal available. I found an airfare for PVG-DXB-MAA, it was $800.00 round trip in economy class. I convinced myself that I could fly in economy because of the airline's outstanding reputation for service the best service in all three of its cabins.

When I completed my work in China, I went to PVG to stay the night in an airport hotel. My flight the next morning was very early. I was surprised that this hotel had a round bed and a view of the airport runways. It was only the second time in my life that I had slept in a round bed. I didn't sleep well the first time in a round bed and this time was no different.

It was early morning when I walked to the airport terminal, and it almost seemed like the peak hours with so many travelers. The check-in was uneventful and I was ready to pass through security within a few minutes. I was surprised to see a credit card affiliate lounge that I was able to get into before the flight. It was a new experience for me and I enjoyed the Chinese hospitality which sometimes can be nonexistent in the airports.

When the time came for me to board the airplane, it was an orderly process that seemed to flow nicely. This was not the norm for me when traveling on flights to or from China, and for that matter within China. When I found my seat, I was surprised to find a nice pillow, blanket, and mini amenity kit. I imagined that these amenities were reserved for the premium classes only. The seat was comfortable and seemed to have ample leg room as well. The meal service was refined and the flight attendants were attentive. During the flight, I thought to myself that this was what coach used to be like in the USA when I was growing up in the jet age.

The layover in DXB was long enough to spend time walking around the massive shopping mall like terminal. I have to admit that I did find some gifts and souvenirs to bring home from my brief stop in the UAE. I enjoyed seeing people from all over the world shopping for the perfect thing to remind them of their layover.

When I arrived in Chennai, my friend was there to pick me up. It was great to see him and reconnect. We had a great visit and covered a lot of ground while I was visiting him. I was happy that I had brought him a list of things that left space in my suitcase for my new things to go home with me. Despite having the extra room, I bought another suitcase to get everything home. I was thankful for the airline's generous baggage allowance for economy passengers which allowed me to have 3 checked bags.

This story would not be complete without me sharing the adventures of going to the Vankteswara Temple in Tirupati. We were up very early in the morning to board a van that would take us to the temple. I was the only non-Indian making this pilgrimage and I was reflective on what this must have meant to the others on the van. The trip would take us a few hours.

We stopped for breakfast along the way and all of us went into the dining room to find a buffet. We took our plates and made our way down the line, my friend pointed out what each item was when I did not know it. At the end of walk through the buffet, I had an almost full plate of food. When we sat down, I looked around and saw everyone eating with their hands. My friend said he would go and get me a spoon. While he was looking for a spoon, I began to eat with my hands. This surprised both me and my friend who came back with a spoon because I am not a fan of eating with my hands. I made do with it.

When we arrived at the gates and entered the temple grounds, I realized the significance of this trip for my friend. It was very impressive and the building and the architecture made it feel like a sacred place. As we drove closer to the actual temple, I could see more and more people walking around the grounds. This was going to be an experience of a lifetime.

My friend told me that before he entered the temple, he was going to make his way to the room where he would have his head shaved. This is something he had done on each and every trip to the temple. It was considered a donation to the temple. He mentioned this to me in the van on the drive up and I didn't think I would do it. When he started towards the room, I asked him if it was appropriate for me to have my head shaved and he replied yes.

When we walked into the room, there were men sitting against the wall with straight edge razors and buckets of water next to them. Sitting in front of them were the men who were having their heads shaved clean to the scalp. My friend and I sat in front of a couple of the men and in a matter of minutes, my head was shaved bald.

On our way to the showers, they gave us each a tiny bar of soap. I remember I was in my shower stall next to my friend's stall getting ready to wash up when I felt the water hit my bare head. I had no idea it would feel that way, it was intense. When I put the bar of soap on my bare scalp with my hand, I could feel it. I said to my friend in the next shower stall over that my head felt like elephant hide. I was surprised it was not soft like I imagined it would be. I made peace with it, knowing that my hair would grow back quickly. My hair did grow back quite a bit by the time I was ready to leave India.

When I arrived at the airport for my flight in the middle of the night, I was somewhat sleepy. I checked in quickly and when the ticket counter agent handed me my boarding card, I did a double take. I always know my seat number for my flight and when I looked at the seat number, I knew this was not my original seat number. I said to the agent that there was an issue with my boarding card and told her that I did not think that this was my seat. She said that is what is in the record as that seat and it is in first class. I woke up quickly when she said that to me. I told her that I didn't understand how I went from economy to first class. She said the airline must have granted me an upgrade. Rather than ask on what basis, I said thank you and asked her for directions to the lounge.

When I got to the lounge, I looked at both of my boarding cards before I put the DXB-PVG one in my wallet. I was still dumbfounded that I was in first class MAA-DXB. What came next was nothing short of a road warrior miracle. The boarding card for DXB-PVG showed that the seat was in business class. I enjoyed a drink and a light snack before I made my way to the gate.

I boarded the plane and found my way to my first class seat, which up until then, was one of the most luxurious seats I had ever flown in. It was massive and oversized. I quickly made friends with one of the flight attendants, when I told her my story of how I ended up in this seat. She was very attentive throughout the flight and gave me an amazing first class experience.

When I arrived in DXB for my layover, I looked for the business class lounge and found it was on the second floor. It was almost half the size of the terminal and seemed to stretch forever. I walked it twice before I formed my plan of attack. I enjoyed a 5-star brunch in the dining hall complete with more cutlery than a family of four could use all together during one meal. I was in airline lounge heaven!!!

I finished my brunch and walked until I found a more secluded area of the lounge that was clearly designed for kids. They had doughnuts with every imaginable topping including sprinkles, nuts, and candies. There was ice cream in the cups like I had when I was in school or during intermission in the theaters in London. My inner child was jumping for joy inside my grown up body!!!

The time came for me to leave the lounge, I felt like I was saying goodbye to a good friend when I left the lounge. I was sad at the thought that I would never experience a lounge like this again. I am happy that that thought did not come true, I flew SAT-IAH-IST-BCN a few years later and the lounge in IST was equally as impressive in every way!!! I made my way to my gate.

I enjoyed the service in business class on my flight DXB-PVG. While in-flight, I reflected while on what a great opportunity I had had with flying in all 3 cabins of service on this first trip with this airline. I was able to experience everything the airline had to offer in flight and in their premium cabin lounges. It was one of the best travel surprises of my life.

Reflections

How do you experience surprises?

What are some of your favorite memories of surprises?

How will you look at surprises now?

Chapter 10

What I Learned about Endurance-1B 1D

In May 2014, I attended an International Conference in Hong Kong. I had been to Hong Kong in the fall of 2003 so I knew I was in for an interesting experience blending the best of Britain with the best of China. When it came time for me to book the airfare, I remembered that there was a flight schedule that had been on my bucket list for about 10 years.

I was eager to fly the route SAT-IAH-HNL-GUM-HKG and proceeded with booking it. It would be about 30 hours en route which seemed manageable given that I had flown some of the longest non-stop flights on record. It would be 4 legs vs the 2 that would have been possible with a west coast connection.

I was more excited than usual on my travel day knowing that I was going to check off a bucket list item at the end of this long travel day. I had taken the flight between SAT-IAH so many times by this time that it seemed like a commute from one side of town to the other. There was no real thrill about this flight by now, so I was focused on the other 3 legs.

I remembered being on the IAH-HNL in May 1991 when it was a relatively new route. It was great to get on the airplane in IAH and land in HNL non-stop. My previous trips to Hawaii involved at least one layover with a connection. I settled in for the flight in 1B and was eager to be in Hawaii in 8 hours, even if only for a quick 1-hour layover.

When we landed in HNL, I deplaned. I could feel the fresh air in the open terminal and it felt wonderful. I quickly made my way to the next flight's gate with little time to spare. The time I did have to spare, I bought a couple of gifts. I was less than half way to HKG and I was running on lots of adrenaline.

I boarded the airplane in HNL and immediately noticed that it was an old one that had not been updated. It was like going back in time to see the dated seats and interior decor. This 1B was from a bygone era. It was an added bonus to feel nostalgic on this flight HNL-GUM.

This was the 2nd longest flight of the trip with an expected 8 hours flying time. I had flown many of the longest non-stop flights on record, but I had not flown long hauls like this back to back. It felt different on my body about half way to GUM. I was starting to feel fatigued and lethargic. This surprised me given my stamina and endurance while traveling previous long haul flights.

When we arrived in GUM, the captain made an announcement asking the passengers to remain in their seats until he turned off the seat belt sign. He told us that there was a fallen soldier on board that would need to be taken off first with his family. I watched the family walk by me towards the door. I felt an overwhelming sense of grief and gratitude for their sacrifice.

The process of taking the fallen soldier off of the airplane took almost an hour. My layover was only an hour so I knew that I had to go directly to the next gate to board my final flight. As I walked by the gift shops, I thought I don't even have time to buy my mom some postcards, which was something I did at every airport or city that I visited while traveling.

It was a good thing that the airport was small and only a few of us were connecting to the flight to HKG. The gate agent was waiting for us and whisked us onto the airplane. We all boarded the Boeing 737 and within minutes the door was closed and we were on our way.

The flight time between GUM-HKG was a relatively short 5 hours and I thought I had it made. Little did I know that I would hit the wall mid-flight. I was restless and fatigued at this point and still had almost 3 hours in flight. It got the better of me and I decided to get up and stand near the galley area by the door.

There were 3 flight attendants in the galley area when I went up there to stand. One greeted me with a big smile and asked me how I was doing. I told her that I had just hit the wall after flying from SAT earlier this morning. She was kind and told me that she understood. We talked for a little while and I forgot about my fatigue and exhaustion.

During our conversation, she talked with me about the connection time in GUM being so tight because of the fallen soldier coming off the airplane with his family. We both felt emotional about it. She said that she had seen it too many times during her career as a flight attendant. I told her that it was my first experience and it was overwhelming.

As we continued to talk, she told me that she was from Guam and that gave me the opportunity to talk with her about the island in more detail. She was very friendly and was very proud of everything that Guam had to offer to both the residents and visitors. I told her that I was disappointed that I did not have time to pick up some postcards for my mom and added that it was for a good reason. She then asked if she could send me some postcards for my mom. I was taken aback at her kindness. I told her that if it was not too much trouble, that would make my mom very happy. She insisted that I give her my address and I did.

After spending some time talking with her, I was ready to go back to my seat 1D for the final couple of hours in flight. It was refreshing once again to meet a caring flight attendant in flight. I made sure to give her my address before I left the airplane. A few weeks later an envelope arrived from the flight attendant with 6 Guam postcards in it for my mom.

The approach into HKG at night was spectacular with all of the lights from the buildings. I could see the shoreline and the massive skyscrapers along it. I was more than ready to be on the ground and get to my hotel. I was glad it was already night and I could go to sleep when I got settled into the hotel.

As I left the airplane, I thanked the flight attendant for getting me past the wall and for being so kind to me. She told me that she enjoyed meeting passengers like me who had a passion for travel and who appreciated the work that the flight attendants do on every flight. We almost hugged as I made my way off the airplane.

After I was checked into the hotel and in my room, I let out a massive sigh. I had made the entire trip from SAT-IAH-HNL-GUM-HKG and could now tick it off my bucket list. I was more tired from this trip than I had been in a very long time.

I thought about the stamina and endurance that it took to be a Global Road Warrior and was pleased with myself for still having it at my age. I had that feeling you get when you face a big challenge and you succeed with it, those feelings of having more confidence in yourself and more self-assurance of what you are capable of doing no matter what comes your way.

I have to admit that I was a bit naive going into this long travel day thinking it would be a piece of cake, only to find out it challenged me both physically and emotionally. I was proud of myself for going after something and making it happen.

I appreciated learning more about myself in terms of my stamina and endurance from this trip. They would go on to serve me well for another 3 years of grueling travel schedules. That trip prepared me for the odd and challenging flight schedules in South America later that summer. One flight in particular departed at 3:30AM and the layover for the connection was 3 hours after a 3 hour flight. I completed the trip with flying colors because the SAT-IAH-HNL-GUM-HKG had built up my travel stamina and endurance.

Reflections

How do you build your stamina and endurance?

What challenges your stamina and endurance?

How can you be more mindful of stamina and endurance in your life?

Chapter 11

<u>What I Learned about Longevity-8D</u>

After the International Conference in Hong Kong was finished, I traveled to mainland China for a couple of weeks of work. At the end of my work time in China, I returned to HKG for my flights home to SAT. It was going to be another long trip to get back home and this time I was going to fly a more direct route.

When I planned this trip, I made the outbound flight a trip of a lifetime that would check off another one of my bucket list items. The multiple flights made up the outbound itinerary SAT-IAH-HNL-GUM-HKG. The return flight would check off another bucket list item for a second time.

The top 10 longest commercial flights list has changed a lot in just the past 5 years. The longest flight on the list as of May 2018 is SIN-EWR at nearly 19 hours. In 2014, the HKG-

EWR flight was on the top 10 longest commercial flights list at almost 16 hours in duration. I had flown on one of the top 10 longest flights in 2009 BOM-EWR which was about 16 hours long.

I knew when I booked the return flights that I would be ready to get home after being on the road for about 3 weeks. With this in mind, I booked the HKG-EWR flight to get me home which had the shortest travel time.

The time came for me to fly PEK-HKG so that I could connect with my HKG-EWR flight. I remember a time when the PEK or HKG airports intimidated me and now I was walking through them with the confidence of knowing where I was and where I was going. It was great to have conquered so many of the major international airports, especially the ones in Asia with their massive crowds.

I watched the flight crew come to the gate and then go onto the airplane while I was at the gate waiting to board the flight. I did not recognize any of them and smiled when I thought to myself, I wonder which ones will be my new friends before we land in EWR.

At this point, as a Global Road Warrior, I was looking for anything to change up the routine on my flights. When I selected my seats at the time I booked the flights, I thought it might be fun to sit in the second cabin instead of the first one. I decided to be radical and sit in the last row middle aisle seat 8D. It would give me a bird's eye view what was going on during the flight.

When it came time to board the airplane, I was eager and ready. After I walked down the jet way, I walked into the airplane with a warm greeting from the International Services Manager. She was pleasant and smiled while she welcomed me on board.

When I walked to my seat, I noticed a placard on the wall outside the second galley. It had an image of the past CEO/President of this airline who had led it out of a disastrous financial situation. He had led the airline from last place to first place with his turnaround plan. I am a huge fan of his leadership practices and business acumen. I was excited to be on the airplane that the airline had dedicated to him.

I got to my seat 8D and settled in and I completed my pre-flight routine. I was welcomed on board by a flight attendant and we chatted briefly. She told me that she was helping with the pre-flight service and that she would not be my flight attendant once we were in the air. I thanked her for telling me and told her I was glad she told me before I got too attached to her. She laughed at my joke, I was going to miss her.

The gentleman in the seat next to me came on with his wife and he said goodbye to her as she kept going to her seat in the cabin behind the curtain. I saw this a lot where couples would fly in separate cabins, so it was not out of the ordinary.

I noticed the woman on the aisle across from me was settling into her seat and saying goodbye to her traveling companion who was going behind the curtain as well. I thought it was odd to see this both next to me and across from me.

The time finally came for us to leave the gate and to start to make the long flight to EWR. Once we were up in the air, the flight attendants came out to start the service. My flight attendant was the ISM. I had not seen the ISM assigned a service zone on any of my previous flights and asked her about it. She told me that it was one of the changes from the merger, the ISMs had a service zone on all international flights along with their other duties. She was very professional about how she explained it to me.

During our talk, I got the scoop on some more of the changes that came with the merger. She casually mentioned that she had been around for a very long time and that she had seen so many changes over the years. I said that it was my experience during my career that change was a constant and those who went with it fared well.

Her service was very good and in some ways reminded me of some of the things that the flight attendants did back in the day. I am talking about the extraordinary service that comes from loving your job and having done it for so many years. I felt very fortunate having her as my flight attendant for this flight.

The meal service was going really well when I looked next to me and saw the woman was talking with the man in the seat. They were not speaking English so I could only watch out of the corner of my eye while not understanding a word being said. All of a sudden he got up and went behind the curtain, and then she sat down.

When my flight attendant, Ellen, came back to serve my main course, she did a double take when she saw the woman was in the seat. What she did next was worth the price of the ticket. Her professionalism was on point. She told the woman that she could not change seats mid-flight and that she had to return to her ticketed seat. She escorted her to her to seat and came back with the man.

The woman came back up again a little later to talk with her husband and ended up sitting in his lap for a few minutes before Ellen came out of the galley. She told them sternly that this was the last time that she was going to talk with them about staying in their ticketed seats. The woman got off of his lap and went back to her seat. That was the last time anything needed to be said to either one of them.

As if this was not enough of a show, I saw another one happening across from me. The woman sitting on the aisle across from me left her seat and went behind the curtain. A little while later, her traveling companion came and sat in the seat. She did this just in time for the mid-flight snack service.

When Ellen came to her seat to ask her if she wanted a snack, she did a double take again. This time was more entertaining than with the seat swappers because the women looked enough alike that a first glance, you could tell Ellen thought she was seeing things. She politely asked the woman, where is the passenger who was in this seat before? She told her that she was in her seat in the back. Ellen was on it with her special brand of professionalism that would not be impacted by these shenanigans.

When my cabin mates were finished with the in-flight entertainment playing musical chairs, I made my way up to the galley. There were a couple of flight attendants in the galley that asked me if I wanted anything, I declined and responded that I was going to stand up for a little while.

One of the flight attendants and I started talking and gossiping. She laughed when I told her about my cabin mates trying to pull one over on Ellen. I told her that I was impressed with the way she handled them. During our conversation, she told me that Ellen was not about to put up with that kind of misbehaving. I told her that I got the sense from watching her that she was no nonsense when came to playing games with her on her flight. She nodded and said you better believe it.

What I learned about Ellen next caught me off guard completely. Lisa, my flight attendant friend and fellow gossiper, told me that Ellen was the number 1 flight attendant for this airline. I was shocked and at the same time, it made sense to me. She had that jet age persona about her that reminded me of the 'stewardesses' I flew with when I was growing up". I told Lisa that Ellen was humble and understated when she told me that she had been flying for a long time.

After my enjoyable conversation with Lisa, it was almost time to get ready for the meal service before we landed in EWR. That meant I needed to get out of her way and go back to my seat. Much to my glee, I found the appropriate cabin mates sitting next to me and across from me. There was not going to be a second act with Ellen on duty.

Ellen came out and started the service. When she made it to my seat, I said to her that I was honored to be served by such an esteemed and respected flight attendant. I told her that I had found out that she was the number 1 flight attendant with this airline and she smiled brightly.

I told her that I had flown a lot during my life time and that I had flown with many of the original Pan Am '"stewardesses' in the last few years going back and forth to China. I went on to tell her that I felt like there was something unique about her during the service earlier and now it made sense to me. She had a nostalgic way about her that was professional and friendly. She appreciated my compliments and we talked off and on in between the service until she had to get the airplane ready to land.

One thing that stood out from our conversation was that this was her first flight of the new year in May. I asked her how that could be and she told me that she took a world cruise every year starting in January, so in essence she did not fly the first quarter of the year. Ellen's longevity had paid off rather well for her. She was able to cruise around the world each year before starting her work year.

At the end of the flight, Ellen and I talked one last time before we landed and I left the airplane. I told her that being on this flight was a bucket list item for me because it was on the list of the top 10 longest flights. I had no idea being on this flight would be another bucket list item that I had not even thought about. I was on the same flight and was served by the number one flight attendant for this airline. When I told her that, she smiled and thanked me.

By my recollection, Ellen began flying in 1957 which was the year before I was born. I don't know if she is still flying or not in 2018; what I do know is that they don't make them like Ellen anymore. She began her career as the jet age took off when air travel was a glamorous and elegant experience. I love how things lined up for me to meet her and spend some time getting to know her while listening to her stories. Her professionalism and longevity make her a one-of-a-kind flight attendant.

Reflections

How do you show others your professionalism?

What long term commitments have you made in your life?

How can you be more professional?

Chapter 12

What I Learned about First Times-1B

In August 2013, my mom and I were about to embark on a trip of lifetime together. This was a trip that was on my mom's bucket list-she called hers a pale list. She was making her first ever trans-Atlantic flight with me SAT-IAH-LHR. We had planned an itinerary that included visiting 8 countries on 2 continents by air, train, and sea.

I was very excited for my Mom to experience so many things for the first time. It caused me to reflect on many of the things we were about to do on this trip. Many of the things that she was going to do for the first time; I had done many times already. I thought to myself, I want to experience these things with my Mom just like they were my first time all over again.

I had already flown on the Boeing 787 by the time we were on this trip. It was exciting to see

Mom board and settle into her seat 1A. She was like a kid in a candy shop. She explored her seat and asked me how it would make a flat bed. Before I could say anything to her, she almost had her head on the footrest. I told her that it would recline and that her feet would go there, not her head. We laughed.

I remembered my first few times in business class traveling overseas and not knowing what did what. I asked questions and watched what others were doing before I would figure it out for myself. My mom figured things out quickly and was settled in for the long flight.

She was impressed with the meal service and it was fun to see it through her eyes after experiencing it so many times before. I told her to expect the ice cream sundaes next and she said, she would pass on having one. I said "not me" with a smile on my face.

When the flight attendant came to our seats with the dessert cart, she asked Mom if she wanted an ice cream sundae. What came next was priceless. Mom replied "No, thank you " and then without missing a beat, she asked if she could have a warm cognac instead. The flight attendant said yes and brought her one immediately. I looked at my mom and said, "Are you kidding me?"

I have flown nearly a million miles on this airline and I have never seen anyone ask for a warm cognac. It was the first time and it was my mom asking for it. We enjoyed the rest of the flight and landed in London the next morning. We made our way to the hotel that I handpicked for Mom on a previous trip to London. It was in the backend of Mayfair close to pubs, food markets, public transportation, and the Hop on Hop off bus stop. Mom got settled into her room before we went out to explore the area within walking distance. She liked the location a lot.

We had a pub lunch in a very well-known pub near the Baker Street Tube Station. My weekend with Mom in London was off to a good start. We had a booking for high tea in one of the most well-known and traditional tea rooms in London for Sunday afternoon which was located in Mayfair. It was my first time to have high tea in London despite all of my previous trips. We had a fun time enjoying our tea time together. We packed a lot of fun and first time experiences into our weekend in London.

By the time I left on Monday morning for my work week in central UK, I was convinced that she was in good hands with the hotel and pub staff. I would be back to pick her up on Friday afternoon so we could go to the airport hotel for our overnight stay before our early morning flight on Saturday morning LHR-FRA-BCN.

We landed in Barcelona at midday and made our way to the cruise port directly for embarkation. We were both very excited about the cruise that would take us to Italy, France and Tunisia. It was our first cruise together and we did well traveling together in the same mini-suite cabin for the week.

Mom and I were in for an adventure on this cruise line, it was a Spanish-owned line and the primary language on board was Spanish. I was going to be okay since I spoke Spanish and I told Mom I would let her know if there were any important announcements. She smiled and nodded throughout the muster drill and no one was the wiser that she did not understand a word of the emergency procedures.

When the cruise was finished, we made our way to the airport for our flights to Stockholm for the final weekend BCN-OSL-ARN. It was my first time in Scandinavia and it was everything I expected beautiful, clean, safe and outrageously expensive. I paid about $55.00 USD a piece for t-shirts. This was a first that I was not looking forward to repeating.

The day came for Mom and I to fly home and I made our return itinerary with a longer than usual layover in Chicago. We would have lunch downtown before our connecting flight. However, the flight from LHR-ORD was not up to the standard level of service that I was used to from this airline. The flight attendant came to our seats 10KL and asked us what we wanted for breakfast. Mom ordered and then I said that I would like to have the cereal, which was a first for me. She abruptly told me that there were no more cereals and asked me what my second choice was. I asked her politely if she could you get a box of cereal from an economy tray. She huffed and said that she would see what she could do for me. Really?!!! Clearly my elite frequent flyer status meant nothing to her.

She came with Mom's meal and placed it on her tray. She told me that she took a crew meal to make sure I got my cereal. I thanked her and thought to myself, did she really have to point that out to me? Was I taking food from the mouths of others? It was a first; it was one of the worst service experiences. Did I mention that she was the International Services Manager?

By the time Mom and I arrived home in SAT, we both had had our fill of first times and we were ready for something familiar like our own beds and mom's cooking. The first trip of a lifetime from Mom's bucket list would lead us to more firsts that we would experience together. Over the next 4 years, we went on an annual cruise that included firsts for both of us.

Together, we cruised to Alaska, the Panama Canal, and New England and Canada, and Hawaii for the first time. I am certain of one lesson learned from my travels with my mom, and that is that we stay young when we are willing to muster up the courage to do things for the first time. It was amazing to see the Panama Canal for the first time. I know that I look at first times in my life with an open mind and loving heart as a result of the adventures with Mom.

Reflections

How do you experience first times in your life?

What do you like most about first time experiences?

How will you embrace first time experiences going forward?

About the Author

Phil was born during the Jet Age and he has had a passion for travel from a young age. His first flight with his mom and younger sister, was in 1963 when he was 4. His mother tells the story of his first flight with a mom's pride for his confidence and being well-behaved. Over the years, that childlike excitement and enthusiasm has not waned for him.

Phil was fortunate enough to have traveled quite a bit by the time he was an adult. He was a natural adventurer and explorer. Everything changed for him when he officially caught the bug at age 23. He went to The Bahamas for the first time and got a taste of what it was like to travel outside of the USA. From that first trip, he went on to visit more than 80 countries and 6 continents.

Phil was a Domestic Road Warrior in the 1990s. The roles he had in his career during that time supported his desire to make a difference in the lives of the people that he worked with in numerous cities. Phil's passion for people and travel were ignited during that time in his career.

Phil was a Global Road Warrior in his 50s and he was a natural when it came to working in other countries. He had a keen sense of seeking to understand what was important to those he was working with in countries outside of the USA. As he made more trips for his career and vacations, Phil's role transformed to Global Citizen.

Phil has worked in China, Japan, India, Brazil Argentina, Peru, Bolivia, Peru, Spain, UK, and the Czech Republic. Each of these countries and cultures gave Phil a better sense of how to work with anyone anywhere in the world.

Phil worked for several Fortune 200 companies during his 35 year career. His focus throughout his career was on Business Process Improvements and Leadership Development.

Phil's passion for both of these led him to launch his own business consulting and leadership coaching company in early 2018 named Seed and Lead. He is an enthusiastic and engaging consultant and coach who can be counted on to deliver successful results for his clients.

Phil's Harvesting Profits System was designed to support entrepreneurs and business leaders in decreasing costs, increasing profits, and growing their sustainable business model. The HPS was developed as a result of Phil's 35 years of corporate leaderships experiences. An important complement to the HPS is the LEADERS!!! leadership development model. This model focuses on serving leaders as they grow and develop the 7 essential leadership traits. Both the HPS and LEADERS!!! programs produce successful results.

Please visit www.seedandlead.com for more information about Phil Bohlender and his company Seed and Lead.

With Much Gratitude!!!